INTRODUCTION

INTRODUCTION

Change is with us and will always be here, and there are two ways of dealing with it:

- **Reactively,** by responding only when one has to, usually too late

- **Proactively,** by planning for change and trying to keep, if not one step ahead, then at least in the vanguard of change

Of course, there is a third option - ignore it and hope it will go away. This was the course followed by dinosaurs, dodos and many companies that could not read the writing on the wall (eg: British motor bike manufacturers which were devoured by the Japanese onslaught).

CONTENTS

INTRODUCTION 1
How we do or don't react, what this book seeks to achieve

WHAT IS CHANGE? 5
Definitions, incremental change, change drivers, the reasons why organisations change - examples

PREPARING FOR CHANGE 23
Commitment, positioning, expert views, the `SUCCESS' principle, barriers, culture, dealing with negative and positive response, organisational readiness, case studies

MAKING CHANGE HAPPEN 69
Key steps (analysis, design, planning, implementation), a team approach to managing change, dealing with resistance

COMMUNICATION 91
The 5 Ws - to avoid misunderstanding

EPILOGUE 99
How to be SMART and not STUPID, tips, further reading

Dinosaurs died out! Mammals did not!

Instead they embraced change and survived.

INTRODUCTION

Change and change programmes are, however, necessarily difficult and complex to manage, and even, sometimes, to understand.

The objective of this book is to clarify the key elements in the process, including the problems, pitfalls, solutions and the assistance available to those involved in change programmes. You may be an active participant, or on the receiving end, or you may just wish to understand more about it.

This book will not make you into a change expert but it will, we hope, give a good understanding of the basics and serve as an introduction to the process of change.

WHAT IS CHANGE?

WHAT IS CHANGE?

DEFINITIONS

Noun - Making or becoming different
- Difference from previous state
- Substitution of one for another
- Variation

Verb - To undergo, show or subject to change
- To make or become different

The emphasis is on making something different. This could be a major change or merely incremental. Whichever it is implies a difference:

WHAT IS CHANGE?

ANNUAL CHANGE CYCLE

There is major change all around you.

Each year the earth goes through an enormous change caused by its rotation (more perceptible in some parts than others) which forces responses that are staggering in enormity. For example, deciduous trees shed their leaves and close down for winter, to bloom again in spring; and animals change their coats (mink/ermine).

Think, too, of the way in which we humans have to respond to climatic changes, by varying our clothing at different times of the year or by regulating the heating or air conditioning. Our well-being depends upon managing such changes.

SPRING   SUMMER   FALL/AUTUMN   WINTER

INCREMENTAL CHANGE

The change from manual recording of information (writing) to current laptops with advanced capability is an enormous one. In fact, it occurred incrementally through several steps.

| **Ancient** | **19th C** | **early 1900s** | **mid 1900s** | **1980s** | **1990s** |

Each step is incremental, requiring skills training and capital outlay.

The change in information processing was even greater, from scrolls to libraries to main frames to midis to LANs.

METAMORPHOSIS

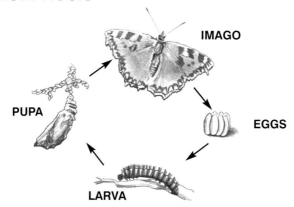

Change can be of an even greater nature. Consider metamorphosis, for example, which requires a complete change of state and represents a severe shock to the status quo (in this case requiring a sleeping phase to cope with the change).

WHAT IS CHANGE?

ORGANISATIONAL

Incremental change:

- <u>10% decrease in staff</u> (usually achieved by natural wastage and early retirement; therefore non-threatening)

- <u>Introduction of performance-related pay</u> (can be threatening for those who might underperform or perceive that they might)

Major change:

- <u>25%+ reduction in staff</u> (commonly involving large-scale redundancies/closures/ relocation and leading to great fear and uncertainty and therefore great resistance)

- <u>Premises rationalisation</u> (usually results in changed work environments in terms of place and benefits)

- <u>Disinvestment/acquisition</u> (usually leads to great fear and uncertainty which can cause it to fail; GEC's bid for Siemens was halted by the staff in Germany fearing for their jobs because of the likelihood of rationalisation)

CHANGE IN BUSINESS

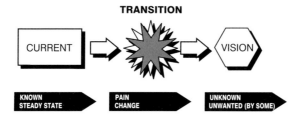

TRANSITION

| CURRENT | → | → | VISION |

| KNOWN STEADY STATE | PAIN CHANGE | UNKNOWN UNWANTED (BY SOME) |

Change management is the process of moving from the current state to the `vision' of the future and involves a degree of transition which may also result in `pain' for some or, more commonly, all.

WHAT IS CHANGE?

WHAT DRIVES CHANGE?

What <u>doesn't</u> drive change is the attitude that, `If it ain't broke, don't fix it'.
Yes, `it' may be working now but is it doing so sufficiently well and will it do so in the future?
You may need to reconsider the meaning of the term `ain't broke'.

Change has many causes, for example:

- Ice Age forced adaptation (hairy mammoth, man discovered how to use caves, skins and fire)

In business change is influenced by, for example:

- New competition
- Price changes
- Technology
- Regulation
- Consumer demand

ADAPT
OR DIE
*COPY, MATCH
OR INNOVATE*

CHANGE DRIVERS

There are many drivers, both internal and external, that force changes on an organisation.

WHAT IS CHANGE?

CHANGE DRIVERS

Factors driving change include:

- New shareholders may force a change as with the Chase Manhattan Bank in 1995

- The appointment of new management almost always causes change as the `new broom sweeps clean'

- Competition may force it, eg: home delivery of fast food (pizza), direct insurance sales or banking

- A change in the market may force it, eg: privatisation, liberalisation of rules (telecoms, UK Stock Exchange, `Big Bang')

WHAT IS CHANGE?

BURNING PLATFORM

Typically there must be a `burning platform' to cause the change to accepted practices.

This phrase comes from the Piper Alpha disaster in the North Sea where the only survivors were those who leapt off the rig **in defiance of instructions** and into the sea which was freezing cold and alight with oil. The burning platform forced a reappraisal of existing rules and the status quo.

For a company, the burning platform could be a combination of things or one overriding concern, eg: disclosure of commissions in Life and Pensions transactions.

WHAT IS CHANGE?

WHY CHANGE?

For your organisation, list the reasons why it might have to change:

HOW TO CHANGE

Having listed the reasons **why** your organisation might have to change, now list **how** it might change:

WHAT IS CHANGE?

WHY CHANGE?

EXAMPLES

Life company

- Increasing competition from banks, direct sales operations
- Disclosure of policy costs to public
- Change by customers to other, unregulated, products

Retailer

- Change in consumer preferences (eg: vegetarianism)
- Climatic changes (warmer winters lead to less demand for, eg: furs)
- Out of town outlets put pressure on smaller independent retailers
- Opening up of the single European market increases competition

WHAT IS CHANGE?

WHY CHANGE?
EXAMPLES

Manufacturer

- Competition has reduced costs by say 35%
- Cheaper overseas producers
- Technological developments render products obsolete
- New environmental/safety rules

Public sector

- Impending privatisation
- Government imposing market forces onto it

WHAT IS CHANGE?

HOW TO CHANGE

EXAMPLES

Life company

- Reduce expenses portion of costs
- Reappraise distribution channels
- Offer new products, form joint ventures

Retailer

- Offer new products, advertise in new markets
- Change stock to reflect environment, change perception of goods to fashion rather than necessities
- Form town loyalty cards, link with others to increase price leverage in purchasing
- Export goods, negotiate with importers so as to offer same goods as competitors

WHAT IS CHANGE?

HOW TO CHANGE
EXAMPLES

Manufacturer

- Review overheads and cut
- Source overseas/invest in technology
- Change products/invest in technology/produce next generation products

Public sector

- Prepare staff by introducing norms and management performance
- Consult staff and explain changes
- Recruit external staff from private sector

No matter which actions are chosen, there are potentially enormous implications. Therefore, there is a need to manage the change in an effective manner.

PREPARING FOR CHANGE

PREPARING FOR CHANGE

MAKING IT HAPPEN

Making change happen involves:

- Moving an organisation's
    - people, and
    - culture

- In line with an organisation's
    - structure
    - processes
    - strategy
    - systems

Such that change is successful and delivers long-lasting benefit to the organisation!

This is not easy and, therefore, requires a process to assist in the management. This is what **Change Management** is all about.

SUCCESSFUL CHANGE MANAGEMENT
COMMITMENT

<u>Successful</u> Change Management is about **taking the people with you**.

DOCK **HMS ORGANISATION** **VISION /
OPPORTUNITY**

Unless the people in an organisation - at all levels, from senior management to employees - are committed to the change, then it will fail. This is not an option and without this commitment any project is doomed.

SUCCESSFUL CHANGE MANAGEMENT

POSITIONING

You must position the change project in the right place to maximise successful implementation.

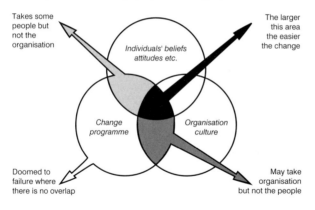

Note: It will be different for different individuals and different parts of the organisation.

SUCCESSFUL CHANGE MANAGEMENT
EXPERT VIEWS

Much research has already been carried out into change.

Several management gurus are recognised; many have distilled their findings down to a number of key points.

Their findings, outlined on the following pages, are not cast in tablets of stone but do serve as useful reminders.

CONDITIONS FOR SUCCESS
EXPERT VIEWS

Rosabeth Moss Kantor is a professor at Harvard who has carried out research into change. These are her 10 Commandments:

1. Analyse the organisation and its need for change
2. Create a shared vision and common direction
3. Separate from the past
4. Create a sense of urgency
5. Support a strong leadership role
6. Line up political sponsorship
7. Craft an implementation plan
8. Develop enabling structures
9. Communicate and involve people
10. Reinforce and institutionalise change

What she is saying is:

- Look at what you have got
- Obtain buy-in at all levels
- Plan the change, and
- Put in place a structure for implementing it
- Finally, make people live and breathe change

CONDITIONS FOR SUCCESS

EXPERT VIEWS

Organisational Development Resources Inc, an American organisation established by Daryl Connor and specialising in change management, has built up an extensive database on change. Its four determinants are:

1   Sponsor commitment
2   Agent skills
3   Target resistance
4   Cultural alignment

The point here is:

- To make sure that there is someone championing the change who has the authority to make it happen

- To put people in place to make it happen

- To concentrate on those who resist most (the other side of the bell curve - see page 90), and

- To try to make the changes in accordance with usual practice, to make people feel as comfortable as possible

CONDITIONS FOR SUCCESS

EXPERT VIEWS

Beckhard, erstwhile professor at M.I.T. (USA), notes seven conditions for success:

1 Organisational vision and direction towards the vision
2 A clear sense of the organisation's identity
3 Understanding of the organisation's external relationships

4 Clear and reachable scenarios
5 Flexible structures
6 Effective use of technology
7 Rewards that harmonise people with the organisation's objectives

The key points here are:

- Understand your organisation and its relationships
- Be flexible

- Have a vision, and
- A map to get there

CONDITIONS FOR SUCCESS
SUMMARY OF EXPERT VIEWS

Each of the gurus has examined change and broadly come to the same conclusions:

- It is very difficult
- The further you go the harder it becomes
- The less that the change has in common with the organisation's culture, the less likely success is
- It needs a strong, important sponsor
- A body of people dedicated to making it happen is essential
- Communication is the key

CONDITIONS FOR SUCCESS
AIDE MEMOIRE

Make sure that your change programme is a **SUCCESS** by following these principles:

Shared vision

Understand the organisation

Cultural alignment

Communication

Experienced help where necessary

Strong leadership

Stakeholder buy-in

CONDITIONS FOR SUCCESS

THE 'SUCCESS' PRINCIPLE

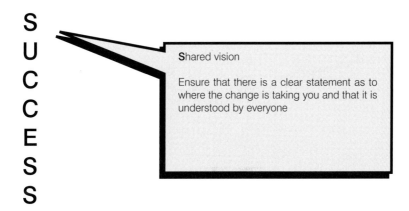

S
U
C
C
E
S
S

Shared vision

Ensure that there is a clear statement as to where the change is taking you and that it is understood by everyone

CONDITIONS FOR SUCCESS

THE 'SUCCESS' PRINCIPLE

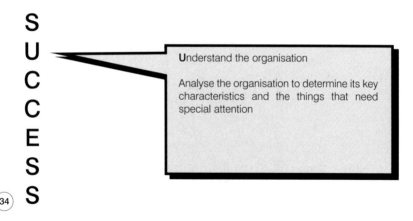

S
U
C
C
E
S
S

Understand the organisation

Analyse the organisation to determine its key characteristics and the things that need special attention

CONDITIONS FOR SUCCESS

THE 'SUCCESS' PRINCIPLE

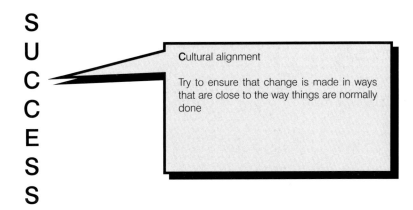

S
U
C
C
E
S
S

Cultural alignment

Try to ensure that change is made in ways that are close to the way things are normally done

CONDITIONS FOR SUCCESS

THE 'SUCCESS' PRINCIPLE

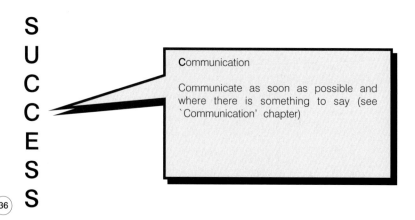

S
U
C
C
E
S
S

Communication

Communicate as soon as possible and where there is something to say (see `Communication' chapter)

CONDITIONS FOR SUCCESS

THE 'SUCCESS' PRINCIPLE

S
U
C
C
E
S
S

Experienced help where necessary

Use appropriate methodologies that have been tried and tested, to ensure that your programme will deliver what you want and not surprises; if this means using external help, then do not be afraid to do so

37

CONDITIONS FOR SUCCESS

THE 'SUCCESS' PRINCIPLE

S
U
C
C
E
S
S

Strong leadership

A strong individual, at the highest level appropriate, must sponsor the change and be seen to do so; the individual must be dedicated to one goal - success of the project

CONDITIONS FOR SUCCESS

THE 'SUCCESS' PRINCIPLE

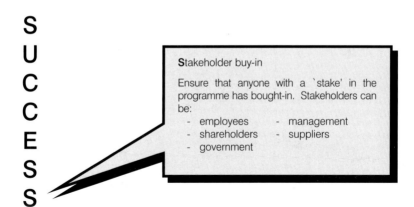

S
U
C
C
E
S
S

Stakeholder buy-in

Ensure that anyone with a `stake' in the programme has bought-in. Stakeholders can be:
- employees
- shareholders
- government
- management
- suppliers

PREPARING FOR CHANGE

BARRIERS

A change programme will affect the way an organisation works. Two factors must be considered **before** implementation:

- Culture
    - how an organisation operates; the change programme will almost certainly be counter cultural in some way

- People
    - how people will receive the change and the actions they might take to resist it

The two are inextricably linked.

BARRIERS

A recent survey in the US* found that the biggest obstacles to change were, in descending order of priority:

- Employee resistance
- Inappropriate culture
- Poor communication/plan
- Incomplete follow-up
- Lack of management agreement on strategy
- Insufficient skills

* *William Schiemann and Associates Inc.*

BARRIERS

Where barriers exist, they must be negated, got round or climbed over. This means understanding the culture, readiness to change and the people.

WHAT IS CULTURE?

- The way that things are done in an organisation (or nation)
- What is acceptable and what is not
- Overt and covert rules/mores/norms that guide behaviour

Compare:

- clearing bank
- investment bank

- civil service
- retail organisation

- nationalised company
- privatised company (in same sectors)

PREPARING FOR CHANGE

WHY LOOK AT CULTURE?

It is important to understand the culture of an organisation in order to understand how best to implement change.

How does culture manifest itself?

Modes of dress (informal, dark suits in the City, less formal suits elsewhere, company uniform)

Attitudes (helpful, couldn't care less, aggressive)

Styles of office/layout (marble banking halls, pristine clear desks, piles of paper, open plan)

Types of buildings (modern, old fashioned, expensive, poorly maintained)

Types of employees (graduates, manual workers, trendy left wing, scientists)

Style of working (clocking on, long hours, extensive travel, etc)

KEY ELEMENTS OF CULTURE

The key elements that influence culture include:

History (long established, new, product of mergers and acquisitions)

Ownership (entrepreneurial, partnership, institution, State, many small shareholders, family, co-operative)

Operating environment (global, national, regional, local)

Mission (profit, charity, growth, loss leader, quality, mutuality)

People (graduates, manual workers, multi-national, accountants, actuaries, salesmen)

Management style (paternal, hire and fire, benevolent, despotic, sharing, controlling)

IT (how relevant is Information Technology to the industry - farming versus telecoms?)

CULTURAL AWARENESS

It is the blend of these key elements that makes up the culture of an organisation and in return may also reflect the culture. The culture must therefore be analysed and understood to enable the change programme to be targeted and to be successful in implementation.

Failure to take culture into account will result in just that - failure! - no matter how well planned or executed a change may be.

TYPES OF CULTURE

Charles Handy in his book `Understanding Organizations' identifies four main types of organisational culture:

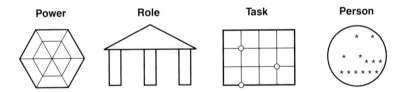

| Power | Role | Task | Person |

TYPES OF CULTURE

Power

This is symbolised by a web, as power flows along the lines to the centre, rather like the vibrations in a spider's web.

Power is wielded by individuals at the centre (eg: well-established entrepreneurial companies or a political party); decisions are easy but may not be right.

Key levers

To change the organisation, you must get the support of the central authority.

TYPES OF CULTURE

Role

This is symbolised by a Greek temple, because it is based on functions and is a very common type where communication flows up (in varying degrees) but never or seldom across (bureaucracy).

Stability is the key and when this goes it falls down, rather like a temple in an earthquake; many organisations fit here.

Key levers

To change this organisation, you must work up each `leg' of the temple, following the structure and protocol. This is not easy and is time consuming. However, it is easier if you have a management structure looking down and across the organisation.

TYPES OF CULTURE

Task

This is symbolised by a net, as power flows up, across and down in a matrix structure.

Jobs are project or task oriented and very flexible with no structure.

Consultancies and some innovative companies are like this; a key feature is customer focused objectives.

Key levers

To change this organisation, you must take the key decision makers with you and gain buy-in from most members.

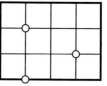

TYPES OF CULTURE

Person

This is symbolised by a cluster or constellation, as individuals are important. Such an organisation is rare and difficult to manage. Some partnerships are like this and professors within academia also fit this profile, getting on with their own interests, taking time out to meet organisational needs.

Key levers

To change this organisation, you must effectively take everyone with you.

PREPARING FOR CHANGE

CULTURE: ORGANISATIONAL ANALYSIS

Describe below the main symbols that reflect the culture of your organisation in terms of:

Modes of dress

Attitudes

Style of office

Buildings

Employees

Style of working

CULTURE: ORGANISATIONAL ANALYSIS

Then analyse your organisation and decide which one of the four cultural examples best fits:

		✔
Power ⬡		
Role 🏛		
Task ▦		
Person ⬤		

This will enable you to understand the **key levers** that will need to be moved if undertaking change. NB: This is a simple illustrative exercise, and more detailed analysis is necessary in a full change programme.

PEOPLE

HOW THEY REACT

- People react differently to change depending on their own persona, circumstances and understanding of the process

- Those opposed to change obviously need attention, but...

- Even those in favour of change will be affected and need to be managed properly

PREPARING FOR CHANGE

PEOPLE

NEGATIVE RESPONSE

Why do people have a negative response to change?

- They cannot see the point of the change (eg: the old guard who have been there for a long time)

- They are too busy (shooting the alligators to help in draining the swamp)

- They are threatened by the change (directly/indirectly)

- They <u>perceive</u> that they are threatened by the change

- Their politics make them natural enemies of the change

- There are cultural problems

Part of change management is identifying these problems and planning to negate them or obviate them.

PREPARING FOR CHANGE

PEOPLE
NEGATIVE RESPONSE

A negative response to change is to be expected. Change is different and many people will be against it on principle, whatever it actually means for them.

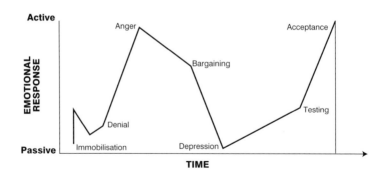

PEOPLE

NEGATIVE RESPONSE

A negative response to change is similar to grieving for the loss of a loved one. The difference may be in the timing and the difficulty of accepting the change; but the emotional responses are the same, requiring **step-handling** to meet each of the changing emotions:

- Immobilisation
- Denial
- Anger
- Bargaining

- Depression
- Testing
- Acceptance

PEOPLE

POSITIVE RESPONSE

Even those in favour of the change - such as those starting a new job, those about to be married, those moving home and (NB: change managers) those on secondment to projects - will need managing to ensure that they do not succumb to pessimism as they move through the different phases.

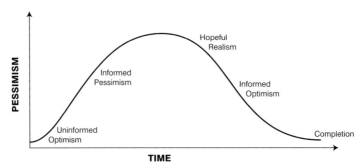

PREPARING FOR CHANGE

PEOPLE
POSITIVE RESPONSE

Reactions will be different at each phase of the change programme:

Uninformed optimism: People are self-confident and positive towards the change

Informed pessimism: People start exhibiting negative responses to change; lose confidence

Hopeful realism: People start to see achievability of change; confidence starts growing

Informed optimism: Confidence returns; people throw themselves into project

Completion: People help rest of organisation; give out confidence

ORGANISATIONAL READINESS TO CHANGE

- Change is difficult; before starting a change programme, it makes sense to assess just how difficult it will be to push through

- The culture of an organisation will affect the ability and speed of an organisation to accept change because it is a way of life

- To change an organisation you must change the people, their beliefs and attitudes and their ways of working; this can be very difficult, especially in strong cultures and often in successful companies (no burning platform)

- It is, therefore, important to understand the readiness of the organisation and management to change

PREPARING FOR CHANGE

ORGANISATIONAL READINESS TO CHANGE
MEASUREMENT

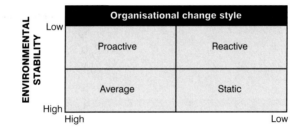

(Based on the work of Harvey and Brown)

ORGANISATIONAL READINESS TO CHANGE

Proactive: These organisations have dynamic management within unstable environments and need to keep one step ahead of the game; change is a way of life for them.

Reactive: These change only when they have to - usually in response to step change in competition and are continually fire-fighting/running to keep still. Change programmes are not usually well executed.

Average: These organisations change enough to keep up with the market - but behind the leaders. Change is difficult but not impossible. Most organisations fit here.

Static: A static organisation usually has a rigid hierarchical style of management which can lead to problems when suddenly the rules of the game change. Change here is extremely difficult to push through.

CASE STUDY 1

QUESTION

A major change programme is about to be initiated in a company. What would be the key steps to be taken up to the announcement?

ANSWER ⟶

63

PREPARING FOR CHANGE

CASE STUDY 1
ANSWER

The steps would include:

- Prepare a communications plan

- Develop questions and answers for top level managers to use when briefing their staff

- Inform major stakeholders

- Brief top level managers and inform them of the timing of the cascade of information down the layers of the organisation

- Issue press release (if appropriate)

- Issue communication to everyone

CASE STUDY 2
QUESTION

An employee has just been seconded to a change programme from his normal job. List below the emotions he might have when he is told, and then describe how to handle them.

_____

_____

_____

How I would handle his emotions:

_____

_____

_____

_____

ANSWER ⟶

65

CASE STUDY 2

ANSWER

The person's reaction to change will be:

- Elation at being chosen coupled with fear for the future post-project

- Concern at the responsibility

- Anxiety about his current reporting relationships

- Lack of certainty regarding his role

- Possible worries about his ability

These concerns can be handled by his current superior giving him a proper briefing and explaining that the secondment represents a vote of confidence in him and his abilities, and by stressing the importance of the project and the role. This would then be followed by a subsequent briefing from the project director along similar lines but in more detail.

CASE STUDY 3
QUESTION

A company has just been acquired. What must the new owners do to ensure a smooth transition period?

ANSWER →

67

CASE STUDY 3
ANSWER

The acquiring company must immediately issue a communication to all staff setting out the blueprint for the future, ensuring that change is kept aligned with the present culture as much as possible. Specifically the company should:

- Explain any immediate changes to operations

- Set out the longer-term plans

- Stress the benefits that are expected to accrue from the acquisition

- Set up briefing meetings and a channel for communications

- Ensure that concerns are met and dealt with sympathetically (the acquisition of Barings Bank where the bonus was maintained is a very good example of this)

MAKING CHANGE HAPPEN

MAKING CHANGE HAPPEN

KEY STEPS

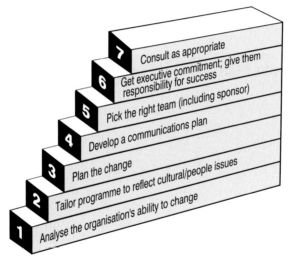

7 Consult as appropriate

6 Get executive commitment; give them responsibility for success

5 Pick the right team (including sponsor)

4 Develop a communications plan

3 Plan the change

2 Tailor programme to reflect cultural/people issues

1 Analyse the organisation's ability to change

MAKING CHANGE HAPPEN

CHANGE MANAGEMENT FRAMEWORK

The key to successful change management is planning.

Planning means thinking through all the issues, all the problems that you might encounter, the steps necessary to deal with them and the choice of team that will be required. If this means getting external help, then do so.

In the following pages we offer a framework to help you in planning your change programme. This can be used for any programme no matter how large or small - the difference will be the extent of the resources and the complexity of the change.

MAKING CHANGE HAPPEN

CHANGE MANAGEMENT FRAMEWORK

This table sets out the key tasks, methods and outputs for a change management programme.

	OBJECTIVES	TASKS	METHODS	OUTPUTS
Analysis (Phase I)	to understand the organisation, its culture and the capacity for change	review: structure, strategy, culture, systems, morale, management practices, external environment	desk research, interviews, workshops, brainstorming	organisational analysis, culture "map", change capacity
Design (Phase II)	to agree the vision, build the team and obtain consensus	develop vision, select team, build buy-in	workshops, meetings, communications	vision, team, consensus, leader/support

Table continued opposite ——→

CHANGE MANAGEMENT FRAMEWORK

	OBJECTIVES	TASKS	METHODS	OUTPUTS
Planning (Phase III)	to plan the realisation of the change	develop plan, build in contingencies, allocate resources, agree timing	desk research, field research, workshops, planning methodologies	plan, risk analysis, dependency chart, agreed resources
Implementation (Phase IV)	to realise the vision by putting the change(s) through the organisation	roll out change across the organisation, communicate to stakeholders, manage risks and dependencies	meetings, actions, team work, workshops, communications	changed organisation, improved performance, survival, changed culture

CHANGE MANAGEMENT FRAMEWORK

Phase I - Analysis

- In this phase it is necessary to understand both the nature of the change and the organisation's culture and its capacity for change

- This will involve carrying out surveys of staff and past projects, and reviewing the structure, strategy, management styles and how the firm interacts with the external environment

Output

- The output from this phase is an understanding of the organisation as it relates to the project and a `map' of the culture

- This should enable you to plan to avoid the potential pitfalls which could arise in the next phase

- Having assessed the change capacity, the pace and scale of change can be optimised

CHANGE MANAGEMENT FRAMEWORK

Phase II - Design

- In this phase of the project the programme is designed; this should be undertaken at a high level and will involve agreeing the precise nature of the vision, building the team to implement the changes and starting to get buy-in from personnel

- The champion should also be agreed at this stage prior to detailed planning; communication, workshops and discussions are critical at this point

Output

- Includes shared vision, team building and agreed responsibilities

CHANGE MANAGEMENT FRAMEWORK

Phase III - Planning

- The objective here is to plan the realisation of the change; this requires looking to the future and thinking through all the risks, dependencies, contingencies and potential problems, and putting together a plan to address them all

- This would include allocating resources, agreeing timing, analysing implications and obtaining buy-in in principle from those affected by talking to them and getting their input

Output

- Will include plans, risk analysis, dependency chart and resources to achieve the plan

CHANGE MANAGEMENT FRAMEWORK

Phase IV - Implementation

- Having put the plan together you must now implement it

- This means ensuring that the plan is followed and that it is re-evaluated in the light of changes to the operating environment and/or strategy and because things crop up which were not foreseen

- The critical skills here are project management and diplomacy; better management of the previous stages will make this stage that much easier

Output

- A well-managed and successful change programme

MAKING CHANGE HAPPEN

IMPLEMENTATION PLAN

PROJECT	JUN	JUL	AUG	SEP	OCT	NOV	DEC	JAN	FEB	MAR	APR	MAY
MOBILISATION												
CHANGE MANAGEMENT (Change management line expanded to demonstrate some key activities)												
Agree communication strategy												
Issue communications												
Agree team												
Hold initial briefing meetings												
Hold workshops												
Re-evaluate change plan												
Make changes and re-brief as necessary												
INFORMATION TECHNOLOGY												
RESTRUCTURE TREASURY												
GL / MIS / BUDGETING												
PROCESS IMPROVEMENTS												
DISTRIBUTION CHANNELS												
"HOUSEKEEPING"												
RE-ENGINEER NEW PRODUCT DEVELOPMENT												
MARKETING												
PROGRESS MEETINGS	☆	☆	☆	☆	☆	☆	☆	☆	☆	☆	☆	☆

IMPLEMENTATION PLAN

The chart opposite shows how change management fits in with a programme and how it is supportive of the larger goals.

Such goals may be to implement: a new IT infrastructure; a radically new organisation; redesigned process; etc.

Whatever the change, it is necessary to integrate the change management into the overall programme.

COMMITMENT

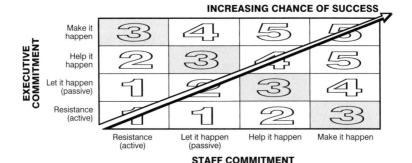

2 or below : forget   **4 or above : success**   **3 : needs work**

Successful project management moves the project from the bottom left to the top right.

TEAM MANAGEMENT

A small dedicated team to manage change can have a major effect on an organisation, one which is disproportionate to the size of the team. Selecting the right individuals is, therefore, critical.

MAKING CHANGE HAPPEN

TEAM MANAGEMENT

ROLES

A number of roles are critical to successful change management. Select the right people or the project will fail. Team numbers will vary depending on project size and duration.

- A senior executive must visibly sponsor the project
- A senior person must take day-to-day responsibility
- A full-time project manager with experience of managing change must run the project (often a role for external consultants)
- Include people with knowledge of the organisation and experience of change programmes (external consultants often involved too)
- Sufficient people at all levels in the organisation must be ambassadors of progress to help spread the word
- Outside consultants can often act as useful catalysts because of their independence

Test proposed team members for appropriateness using some of the many methods available (Belbin, 16PF, Myers-Briggs, ODR, etc). This ensures the correct blend of skills.

TEAM MANAGEMENT
DEVELOPMENT PROCESS

TEAMS

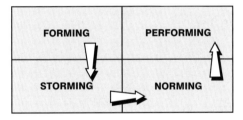

Team members do not usually work well together from day one and have to go through a development process of finding out about each other and achieving a working understanding. Only then will they deliver. The earlier teams form, the quicker they move into productive performance.

TEAM MANAGEMENT
DEVELOPMENT PROCESS

The four development stages that teams go through are generally recognised as follows:

FORMING	PERFORMING
Still a group of individuals; each is trying to set his mark on the group	The desired state cannot be reached until the previous three stages have been completed; very little effective group work will happen until this stage, although individuals may contribute well
STORMING A period of conflict as members get to know each other, egos are bruised and dynamic interplay takes place (needs careful handling to make sure that it is constructive not destructive)	**NORMING** Following the conflict of the previous stage, the group norms and modus operandi are now established

84

REACTIONS TO CHANGE

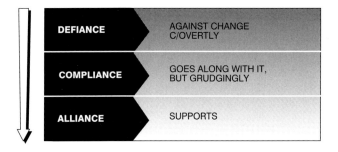

DEFIANCE	AGAINST CHANGE C/OVERTLY
COMPLIANCE	GOES ALONG WITH IT, BUT GRUDGINGLY
ALLIANCE	SUPPORTS

The challenge is to move the organisation and people down the scale.

RESISTANCE

When you come to implement the changes, no matter what you have done to prepare the ground, it will still come as a surprise to many people.

This surprise will turn into resistance quickly and must be managed to ensure success.

Address people's fears to gain their commitment.

RESISTANCE

Resistance is a vote for the status quo and must be dealt with to prevent disruptive behaviour. It must be planned for and handled well, otherwise it will get worse and could damage the project.

> Corporate America is littered with the wreckage of technically sound programs that have been crushed by employee resistance to change
>
> *Tom Terez, Modern Management*

RESISTANCE

REASONS

Resistance occurs for many reasons, both real and supposed:

- Loss of control
- Uncertainty
- Fear of the difference
- Loss of power

- Possible increased workloads
- Threat
- Misunderstandings

A successful change management programme will address these causes and negate them.

MAKING CHANGE HAPPEN

RESISTANCE
HOW TO DEAL WITH IT

Resistance can be overcome when you:

- Involve people in the process

- Train

- Explain the change in easy to understand terms

- Develop shared vision and buy-in

- Explain the reasons (burning platform)

- Address the concerns of stakeholders

- **Above all, communicate**

MAKING CHANGE HAPPEN

RESISTANCE

GAINING ACCEPTANCE

Gaining acceptance goes through the process below, starting with those who are most likely to accept change - innovators - until finally the laggards are won over - or leave.
Use the innovators as Ambassadors of Progress.

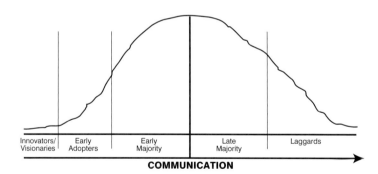

COMMUNICATION

COMMUNICATION

THE FIVE Ws

Who should be told?

When should they be told?

What should they be told?

Where should the message be conveyed?

Who should control the communications process?

Addressing the FIVE Ws is an essential element of a change programme.
Poor communication means that the wrong messages can go out and, therefore,
misunderstandings occur - leading to resistance, antipathy and often failure.

THE FIVE Ws

WHO?

- Everyone who needs to be told about something should be told

- Openness is the key (although there will always be some things which are not disseminated as widely as others)

'Read all about it'

THE FIVE Ws

WHEN?

- Project members must be briefed prior to them joining the project

- All affected employees should be told at the **same** time, to avoid spread of rumours

- Brief those internally before those externally; you don't want staff finding out about change from the media

- Make an announcement following a significant event or decision

COMMUNICATION

THE FIVE Ws
WHAT?

The four rules of communication are:

- Tell `em when you have something to say

- Tell `em what you plan to do

- Tell `em what you are doing

- Tell `em what you will be doing

THE FIVE Ws
WHERE?

- Choose the most effective vehicle to get your message across

- This could be via seminars, staff letters, press releases or whatever; the key is to make sure that your message gets across to the right people, to avoid rumours and hearsay

COMMUNICATION

THE FIVE Ws
WHO SHOULD CONTROL IT?

Usually communications will be under the control of the sponsoring executive.
For a large programme, this is usually the CEO.

It is such an important part of the programme's success that it MUST NOT be left to a junior.

- The project manager will normally have input into it

- Personnel will usually be consulted

- The corporate communications people, if appropriate, will be involved

EPILOGUE

HOW TO SUCCEED

Success in Change Management involves being **SMART**:

Strategy defined

Management buy-in

Assurance to staff

Risk analysis

Time critical implementation

EPILOGUE

HOW TO FAIL

Change Management will fail when you are **STUPID:**

Sponsorship not forthcoming

Team members do not function as agents of change

Unclear vision and commitment

Poorly planned change programme

Inappropriate/insufficient communication

Don't take account of culture

TIPS

Confrontation

Avoid confrontation; obtain a consensus

Manpower changes

Changes in manpower (which often result from change) must be dealt with sympathetically to ensure buy-in and acceptance as well as good morale for remaining staff

EPILOGUE

TIPS

Automation

Bear in mind that automation usually results in manual positions being made redundant

Co-operation and buy-in

It is important that buy-in is obtained from
staff by consensus and not imposition

EPILOGUE

FURTHER READING

`Change Masters', by Rosabeth Moss Kantor, published by Unwin

`Managing at the Speed of Change', by Daryl Connor, published by Villard Books

`The Fifth Discipline', by Peter Senge, published by Century Business

`The Essence of Change', by Liz Clarke, published by Prentice Hall

`An Experiential Approach to Organization Development', by Harvey and Brown, published by Prentice Hall

'Understanding Organizations', by Charles Handy, published by Pelican

'Organizational Transitions', by Beckhard and Harris, published by Addison-Wesley

About the Author

Neil Russell-Jones

Neil, an MBA, is a management consultant. He is a chartered banker and a member of the Strategic Planning Society. He has worked internationally with many organisations, particularly in the areas of strategy, BPR, change management and shareholder value. He is a guest lecturer on the City University Business School's Evening MBA Programme and has lectured and spoken in many countries. He is also an advisor for The Prince's Trust. The numerous articles and books written by  him include three other pocketbooks (on marketing, business planning and decision making), 'Financial Services – 1992' (Eurostudy) and 'Marketing for Success' and 'Value Pricing', both published by Kogan Page and, with 'The Marketing Pocketbook', written in conjunction with Dr Tony Fletcher.

Contact

You can reach the author on this E-mail: neiljones@neilsweb.fsnet.co.uk

THE MANAGEMENT POCKETBOOK SERIES

Pocketbooks

Appraisals
Assertiveness
Balance Sheet
Business Planning
Business Presenter's
Business Writing
Challengers
Coaching
Communicator's
Controlling Absenteeism
Creative Manager's
Cross-cultural Business
Cultural Gaffes
Customer Service
Decision-making
Discipline
E-commerce
E-customer Care
Empowerment
Facilitator's

Handling Complaints
Improving Efficiency
Improving Profitability
Induction
Influencing
Interviewer's
Key Account Manager's
Learner's
Managing Budgets
Managing Cashflow
Managing Change
Managing Your Appraisal
Manager's
Manager's Training
Marketing
Meetings
Mentoring
Motivation
Negotiator's
Networking

People Manager's
Performance Management
Personal Success
Project Management
Problem Behaviour
Quality
Sales Excellence
Salesperson's
Self-managed Development
Starting In Management
Stress
Teamworking
Telephone Skills
Telesales
Thinker's
Time Management
Trainer Standards
Trainer's

Pocketsquares

Leadership: Sharing The Passion
The Great Presentation Scandal
The Great Training Robbery
Hook Your Audience

Pocketfiles

Trainer's Blue Pocketfile of
Ready-to-use Exercises

Trainer's Green Pocketfile of
Ready-to-use Exercises

Trainer's Red Pocketfile of
Ready-to-use Exercises

Audio Cassettes

Tips for Presenters
Tips for Trainers

ORDER FORM

Your details

Name _____

Position _____

Company _____

Address _____

_____

_____

Telephone _____

Facsimile _____

E-mail _____

VAT No. (EC companies) _____

Your Order Ref _____

Please send me:

	No. copies
The Managing Change Pocketbook	☐
The _____ Pocketbook	☐
The _____ Pocketbook	☐
The _____ Pocketbook	☐
The _____ Pocketbook	☐

Order by Post

MANAGEMENT POCKETBOOKS LTD
14 EAST STREET ALRESFORD HAMPSHIRE SO24 9EE UK

Order by Phone, Fax or Internet

Telephone: +44 (0)1962 735573
Facsimile: +44 (0)1962 733637
E-mail: sales@pocketbook.co.uk
Web: www.pocketbook.co.uk

Customers in USA should contact:
Stylus Publishing, LLC, 22883 Quicksilver Drive,
Sterling, VA 20166-2012
Telephone: 703 661 1581 or 800 232 0223
Facsimile: 703 661 1501 E-mail: styluspub@aol.com